The Co-Teaching Lesson Plan Book

Third Edition

by Lisa A. Dieker, Ph.D.

KNOWLEDGE
by Design, Inc.

Whitefish Bay, Wisconsin

The Co-Teaching Lesson Plan Book (3rd ed.).

To obtain permission to use the material from this work, please submit a written request to:
> Knowledge by Design
> Permissions Department
> 5907 N. Kent Avenue
> Whitefish Bay, WI 53217

ISBN   0-9708429-8-8

Printed in the United States of America.

Ordering Information

See the order form on last page of this book or visit our web site: http://www.knowledge-by-design.com/.

About the Author

Lisa Dieker is an Associate Professor at the University of Central Florida. Her research, teaching, and service focus on creating stronger collaborative environments between general and special education teachers. During a recent sabbatical she served as a substitute teacher to utilize and validate the strategies recommended in her book. She has published articles on co-teaching, inclusion, intervention assistance teams, and reflective thinking. She coordinates several field-based grants and has had the opportunity to observe classrooms and consult with teachers throughout the United States.

Author Contact Information:

Lisa Dieker, Ph.D.
Department of Child, Family and Community Sciences
College of Education - 315F
University of Central Florida
P.O. Box 161250
Orlando, FL 32816-1250
email: ldieker@mail.ucf.edu

Acknowledgements

I would like to thank the numerous teachers, administrators and colleagues who have shared ideas and granted me access to their classrooms to develop this book. The ideas presented have all been observed in actual practice.

I want to specifically thank the following people who have contributed to both my knowledge base and with the material in this book. I would like to acknowledge that the following pages have been developed or modified from material presented by my colleagues:
> pp. 2-3 lesson plans were created by Dianne Kelley and Gail Wranovsky
> Week 28 testing ideas were modified from material created by Janet Hill
> Research and development of reflective frameworks modified from my work with Lisa Monda-Amaya.

This book is dedicated to all professionals who value and commit to collaboration between general and special education to ensure the success of all students.

How to Use
The Co-Teaching Lesson Plan Book

Lisa A. Dieker, Ph.D.

Purpose

With the recent changes in the Individuals with Disabilities Education Act (IDEA) related to issues of highly qualified teachers, the use of co-teaching is on the rise at all levels of education. Research has demonstrated that co-teaching is an effective instructional strategy, when implemented correctly, for enhancing the success of students with disabilities in general education classrooms. However, as many teachers have discovered, new tools are needed to support the collaborative planning and communication required to make co-teaching successful.

Current lesson plan structures do not address the needs of both co-teachers. Nor do plan books allow space for planning and documenting individual accommodations for students with disabilities. This book was designed to facilitate collaborative planning between general and special educators and provide documentation of accommodations and modifications made for students with disabilities.

Unique Features

Teachers will appreciate many unique features found in this plan book:
- Creates shared planning by both the general and special educator completing the weekly plan.
- Offers side-by-side view of planning and meeting state standards.
- Allows special educators to document the interventions used, and progress made, toward IEP goals.
- Allows teachers to evaluate, refine, and continue their development as co-teachers.
- Provides notes from the author for insight into the value, art, and the impact of co-teaching.

Features for General Educators

Like most lesson plan books, space is provided to outline lesson activities and assessment procedures for each class subject and period. The general educator uses the left page to record the "big ideas" and goals of each co-taught lesson. This format is easy to implement and requires no additional planning time beyond the time spent with a traditional plan book.

Features for Special Educators

Special educators complete the modified assessments column on the left-hand page of the book for any academic or behavioral needs of a student as well as the right-hand page. The special educator notes the types of co-teaching models the team will use, academic and behavioral adaptations needed for specific students, materials that may be needed to meet all students' needs as well as a place to jot notes to each other or about student performance related to IEP goals and obectives. Using this format ensures that what is special about special education is maintained throughout the co-taught setting.

Outcomes and Benefits

Given concern for the success of all students, space is offered for both teachers to identify students who need additional accommodations or who are at-risk of failing in the class (see top box on each page). Interventions planned by the special educator may be used to assist all students in the class.

As with any plan book, this model only works if both co-teachers are committed to preparing lessons in advance so that they can effectively meet the needs of all students. As a result of using *The Co-Teaching Lesson Plan Book*, you will notice the following benefits:
- Clarified roles of both teachers,
- Combinded ownership of planning,
- Improved instructional planning for meeting the needs of individual students,
- Increased collaboration in lesson development and delivery,
- Improved documentation of the development and use of specific accommodations for reporting IEP progress.

Remember that communication and evaluation are the keys to successful co-teaching relationships. I hope this new structure helps you be more effective as you work together to ensure the success of all students.

Best wishes for a successful and rewarding co-teaching experience!

Sample Co-Teaching Lesson Plans

Note: Below are sample lesson plans to illustrate how the co-teaching planning model can be used across subject areas. In contrast to typical plan books, this plan book is designed for those periods in which teachers co-teach.

Week of _____

Subject _____

Class Hour _____

Strategy Suggestion...

Target Students
_____
_____
_____
_____
_____
_____

Day/Date	Big Idea/Goals	Lesson Activities	Assessment	
			Standard	**Modified**
Language Arts	Students will prepare an oral presentation on a book of their choice. Students will evaluate peers' presentations and provide one constructive comment and one positive comment.	Review book report requirements. Provide students in-class time to prepare report.	5 minute oral presentation with a clear sequence of ideas. Completed evaluations with a minimum of 1 positive and 1 constructive comment.	Provides pictures and 1 sentence statement of each picture. Gave a verbal positive comment to at least one peer following the presentation.
Algebra	Students will multiply the correct terms in a binomial and combine two binomials into a single binomial. Students will use positive language with their peers.	Demonstrate the FOIL method. Assign practice problems for students to complete.	Homework of 20 problems with 90% accuracy. At least 1 positive comment was made during class today.	Complete 5 problems with 80% accuracy. Responded with an affirmation to at least one positive comment made by a peer (e.g., thank you).
Science	Students will be able to use a balance. Students will extrapolate information from observation/data collection. Students will demonstrate appropriate cooperative group behavior.	Students will gather necessary materials (balance, weights, etc.) for the experiment. As a team, students will balance various objects and record data on an observation form.	Data sheet completed for balancing 10 items with 90% accuracy. Peer rating of 4/5 on contribution to group.	Data sheet completed for balancing 5 items with 80% accuracy. Peer rating of 3 or higher on contribution to group.

This page is designed to be completed by the General Educator

Sample Co-Teaching Lesson Plans

Co-Teaching Structures:
- (O) one lead, one support
- (S) station teaching
- (P) parallel teaching
- (A) alternative teaching
- (T) team teaching

			Strategy Suggestion...			Students with Special Needs

Co-Teaching Structure	Academic Adaptiations (as needed for gifted students and students with disabilities)	Behavioral Adaptiations	Materials/ Support Needed	Performance Data and Notes
Alternative teaching	• Allow students to present report using a variety of styles (brown bag report, rap song, note cards, etc.) • Allow students with language issues to present with a peer. • Allow three minute presentations for Sue and Jason.	• Review behavior expectations of audience; provide student with specific checklist to self-monitor behavior.	Provide small group break out sessions to edit, practice, refine, etc.	*We need to talk about Tanya's performance this past week.*
One teach– one support	William will complete one-half of the assignment. Zoe will identify terms for each FOIL.	When frustrated, Alex will be allowed two-minute breaks to regain composure.	Color code FOIL terms. Teacher observation.	*I am worried about too much support for Sally. She does not seem to be learning to work independently.*
Parallel instruction. Monitor students working in collaborative teams.	Jeff and Zoe will be required to record list of materials used. Given a list of objects, Kevin will circle pictures of materials used in lab.	Jerrod's teammates will ask him 5 questions during lab. David will pass out lab materials.	Teacher generated picture worksheet. Peer coaching training.	*IEP goal: When asked a question, student 4 will respond 70% of the time by answering yes or no.* *Remember to record more data on this IEP goal.*

This page is designed to be completed by the Special Educator

As You Begin...

Meeting Agenda
Suggested time: 3 hours

Before you start the new school year I strongly recommend spending, at a minimum, half a day together talking over the following questions:

1. How will we deal with any behavioral issues that arise?

2. How will we deal with grading?

3. Who will contact parents and how will we share and maintain communication throughout the year?

4. Are there accommodations that students will be allowed to use in local and state assessments that we need to incorporate into our daily planning?

Reflective Framework

Here are some questions to guide the development of your classroom structure to ensure the success of both teachers and your students:

1. What do we see as our roles in the classrooms?
2. What do we see as our individual strengths in what we will contribute to all learners?
3. What are our pet peeves about teaching?
4. Will we share teaching space or are there two desk available in the room? If shared, how do we plan to share supplies, passes, and basic materials?
5. When will we have time to plan together?
6. What rules do we want to set related to any planning time we might have? For example, can we agree:
   a. To talk about students individually after we plan for the entire class.
   b. To make certain we arrive at our assigned time promptly with needed materials to make the most use of limited time together.
   c. To create a Plan B about what to do if one of us is out or cannot plan.
7. What if our designated time together is not enough time to plan our lessons effectively? How will we proceed?
8. What is the best thing we anticipate will result from our work together this year?
9. What is our greatest fear about working as a team?
10. How do we plan to introduce ourselves the first day of class?
11. How do we plan to handle any issues of fairness that might arise in the class?

Topics to revisit in our next meeting...

A Note from Author Lisa Dieker

One issue many co-teaching teams fail to address involves informing parents of the new service delivery model in which both general and special education students will be receiving services.

As you begin your planning for the new school year, remember to take time to prepare a letter that you can send home informing parents that their child will receive the benefit of two teachers in your class this year.

Professional Development Resources

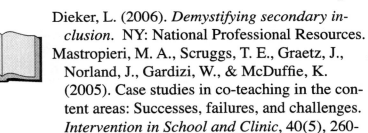

Dieker, L. (2006). *Demystifying secondary inclusion.* NY: National Professional Resources.
Mastropieri, M. A., Scruggs, T. E., Graetz, J., Norland, J., Gardizi, W., & McDuffie, K. (2005). Case studies in co-teaching in the content areas: Successes, failures, and challenges. *Intervention in School and Clinic*, 40(5), 260-270.

Rubistar
http://rubistar.4teachers.org/

Internet4Classrooms
http://www.internet4classrooms.com/

Follow-up To-Do List
General Educator

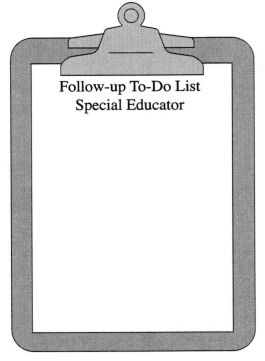

Follow-up To-Do List
Special Educator

Week of _____

Subject _____

Class Hour _____

Strategy Suggestion...
Get acquainted activities – Use these types of activities regularly to help students learn about each other. These types of activities are critical if students with disabilities join the class in the middle of a quarter.

Target Students
_____
_____
_____
_____
_____

Day/Date	Big Idea/Goals	Lesson Activities	Assessment	
			Standard	Modified
Monday				
Tuesday				
Wednesday				
Thursday				
Friday				

This page is designed to be completed by the General Educator

Co-Teaching Structures:

- (O) one lead, one support
- (S) station teaching
- (P) parallel teaching
- (A) alternative teaching
- (T) team teaching

Strategy Suggestion...

Hold classroom forums – Have a box in the back of the room where students or the teacher can place a problem that occurs in their lives. Once a week take 10 minutes to discuss a problem in the box and ask students to share solutions.

Students with Special Needs

_____

_____

_____

_____

_____

Co-Teaching Structure	Academic Adaptations (as needed for gifted students and students with disabilities)	Behavioral Adaptations	Materials/ Support Needed	Performance Data and Notes

This page is designed to be completed by the Special Educator

Week of _____

Subject _____

Class Hour _____

Strategy Suggestion...
Joint projects – Allow students to work together on projects. Assign specific roles to each student.

Target Students
_____
_____
_____
_____
_____
_____

Day/Date	Big Idea/Goals	Lesson Activities	Assessment	
			Standard	Modified
Monday				
Tuesday				
Wednesday				
Thursday				
Friday				

This page is designed to be completed by the General Educator

Co-Teaching Structures:
- (O) one lead, one support
- (S) station teaching
- (P) parallel teaching
- (A) alternative teaching
- (T) team teaching

Students with Special Needs

_____
_____
_____
_____
_____
_____

Co-Teaching Structure	Academic Adaptations (as needed for gifted students and students with disabilities)	Behavioral Adaptations	Materials/ Support Needed	Performance Data and Notes

This page is designed to be completed by the Special Educator

Week of _____

Subject _____

Class Hour _____

Target Students
_____
_____
_____
_____
_____

Day/Date	Big Idea/Goals	Lesson Activities	Assessment	
			Standard	Modified
Monday				
Tuesday				
Wednesday				
Thursday				
Friday				

This page is designed to be completed by the General Educator

Co-Teaching Structures:

    (O) one lead, one support
    (S) station teaching
    (P) parallel teaching
    (A) alternative teaching
    (T) team teaching

Strategy Suggestion...
Daily celebrations of unique talents and strengths – Select something you can celebrate publicly for each student (e.g., student who comes early to class, student who helps others, etc.).

Students with Special Needs
_____
_____
_____
_____
_____

Co-Teaching Structure	Academic Adaptations (as needed for gifted students and students with disabilities)	Behavioral Adaptations	Materials/ Support Needed	Performance Data and Notes

This page is designed to be completed by the Special Educator

Week of _____

Subject _____

Class Hour _____

Strategy Suggestion...
Quote of the day – Use one of your bulletin boards to post interesting quotes collected by students. Quotes must be interesting, humorous, and related to the topic being studied.

Target Students
_____
_____
_____
_____
_____

Day/Date	Big Idea/Goals	Lesson Activities	Assessment	
			Standard	Modified
Monday				
Tuesday				
Wednesday				
Thursday				
Friday				

This page is designed to be completed by the General Educator

Co-Teaching Structures:

- (O) one lead, one support
- (S) station teaching
- (P) parallel teaching
- (A) alternative teaching
- (T) team teaching

	Strategy Suggestion...
	Teach social skills – Write a goal on the board for the day or week (e.g., use positive language) and reward and praise students when they exhibit the skill.

Students with Special Needs
_____
_____
_____
_____
_____

Co-Teaching Structure	Academic Adaptations (as needed for gifted students and students with disabilities)	Behavioral Adaptations	Materials/ Support Needed	Performance Data and Notes

This page is designed to be completed by the Special Educator

Week 4 Co-Teaching Progress Check-up

Meeting Agenda
Suggested time: 30 minutes

Now is a good time to schedule a meeting between co-teachers to reflect on the experience to-date. Use the following agenda to guide the discussion.

1. Discuss each of the questions in the Reflective Framework (below).

2. Read and discuss the Author's Note (next page).

3. Record your thoughts and notes in the space provided for
    - Ideas
    - Topics to revisit in our next meeting
    - Follow-up to-do list for each team member

Reflective Framework

Co-Teaching (Dieker, 2006)

- How will you determine the success of the co-teaching relationship? (i.e., students' grades, personal perceptions, student/parent comments)

- How will you evaluate student learning? Take time now and write a date on the calendar for your next meeting. I recommend meeting at least once a month.

- How will you conduct these evaluations? (i.e., talk in person, send written notes, meet outside of school)

- How will you determine the students' perceptions of co-teaching each semester? (i.e., informational evaluation, interviews)

- How will you keep your administrator involved in the process and assist him/her in evaluating your co-teaching efforts? (i.e., written notes, informal observations, team meetings)

- How will you involve parents in all aspects of the co-teaching relationship? (i.e., letters home, phone conversations, parent meetings)

Topics to revisit in our next meeting...

Professional Development Resources

Dieker, L. & Ousley, D. (2006). Speaking the same language: Bringing together highly-qualified secondary English and special education teachers. *Teaching Exceptional Children Plus*.

Magiera, K. & Zigmond, N. (2005). Co-Teaching in middle school classrooms under routine conditions: Does the instructional experience differ for students with disabilities in co-taught and solo-taught classes? *Learning Disabilities Research and Practice, 20*(2), 79-85.

Power of Two
http://www.powerof2.org/

LD Online
http://www.ldonline.org/

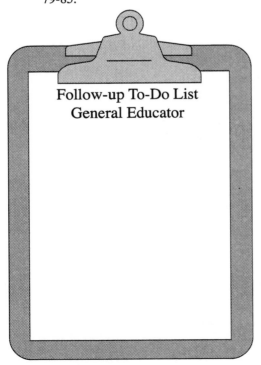

Follow-up To-Do List
General Educator

Follow-up To-Do List
Special Educator

Week of _____

Subject _____

Class Hour _____

Target Students

_____
_____
_____
_____
_____
_____

Day/Date	Big Idea/Goals	Lesson Activities	Assessment	
			Standard	Modified
Monday				
Tuesday				
Wednesday				
Thursday				
Friday				

This page is designed to be completed by the General Educator

Co-Teaching Structures:

- (O) one lead, one support
- (S) station teaching
- (P) parallel teaching
- (A) alternative teaching
- (T) team teaching

Strategy Suggestion...
Base groups – Assign each student a number, letter, and shape. Use these three different variables to assign students to different groups. Consider one of the groupings for ability level tasks.

Students with Special Needs
_____
_____
_____
_____
_____

Co-Teaching Structure	Academic Adaptations (as needed for gifted students and students with disabilities)	Behavioral Adaptations	Materials/ Support Needed	Performance Data and Notes

This page is designed to be completed by the Special Educator

Week of _____

Subject _____

Class Hour _____

Strategy Suggestion...
Assign class roles – Give students roles such as captain, co-captain, recorder, sunshine person, etc. Be certain students with disabilities have the chance to serve in leadership roles.

Target Students
_____
_____
_____
_____
_____

Day/Date	Big Idea/Goals	Lesson Activities	Assessment	
			Standard	Modified
Monday				
Tuesday				
Wednesday				
Thursday				
Friday				

This page is designed to be completed by the General Educator

Co-Teaching Structures:

(O) one lead, one support
(S) station teaching
(P) parallel teaching
(A) alternative teaching
(T) team teaching

Students with Special Needs
_____
_____
_____
_____
_____

Co-Teaching Structure	Academic Adaptations (as needed for gifted students and students with disabilities)	Behavioral Adaptations	Materials/ Support Needed	Performance Data and Notes

This page is designed to be completed by the Special Educator

Week of _____

Subject _____

Class Hour _____

Target Students
_____
_____
_____
_____
_____

Day/Date	Big Idea/Goals	Lesson Activities	Assessment	
			Standard	Modified
Monday				
Tuesday				
Wednesday				
Thursday				
Friday				

This page is designed to be completed by the General Educator

Co-Teaching Structures:

(O) one lead, one support
(S) station teaching
(P) parallel teaching
(A) alternative teaching
(T) team teaching

Strategy Suggestion...

Clear the air – Students are given a piece of paper to write down anything that is bothering them. Place a star in front of any item that they only want the teacher to read. The teacher selects items without stars to read to the class; the entire class discusses possible solutions.

Students with Special Needs
_____
_____
_____
_____
_____

Co-Teaching Structure	Academic Adaptations (as needed for gifted students and students with disabilities)	Behavioral Adaptations	Materials/ Support Needed	Performance Data and Notes

This page is designed to be completed by the Special Educator

Week of _____

Subject _____

Class Hour _____

Target Students
_____
_____
_____
_____
_____

Day/Date	Big Idea/Goals	Lesson Activities	Assessment	
			Standard	Modified
Monday				
Tuesday				
Wednesday				
Thursday				
Friday				

This page is designed to be completed by the General Educator

Co-Teaching Structures:

- (O) one lead, one support
- (S) station teaching
- (P) parallel teaching
- (A) alternative teaching
- (T) team teaching

Students with Special Needs

_____
_____
_____
_____
_____

Co-Teaching Structure	Academic Adaptations (as needed for gifted students and students with disabilities)	Behavioral Adaptations	Materials/ Support Needed	Performance Data and Notes

This page is designed to be completed by the Special Educator

Week 8 Co-Teaching Progress Check-up

Meeting Agenda
Suggested time: 30 minutes

Now is a good time to schedule a meeting between co-teachers to reflect on the experience to-date. Use the following agenda to guide the discussion.

1. Discuss each of the questions in the Reflective Framework (below).

2. Read and discuss the Author's Note (next page).

3. Record your thoughts and notes in the space provided for
   - Ideas
   - Topics to revisit in our next meeting
   - Follow-up to-do list for each team member

Reflective Framework

As the first quarter draws to a close, now is a good time for a conversation about cooperative teaching and grading. Use the following discussion questions to guide the conversation:

Cooperative Teaching (Dieker, 2006)
- Do we both feel comfortable in our roles in the classroom today?
- What were the successes of today's lesson?
- What do we both see as areas that need to be addressed in future lessons?
- Who will be responsible for implementing these changes?
- Was consensus reached with regards to the final decision?
- Are there any collaborative issues that we should address to improve our collaborative relationship? (i.e., time, grading, role clarification, parental contact, assessment, etc.)

Grading (adapted from Meltzer, et al, 1996)
- Are you explicit about the grading policy?
- Do you use multilevel grading?
- Do you give credit for participation?
- Do you evaluate students' performance in a variety of ways?
- Do you embrace multiple intelligences?
- Do you evaluate social skills?
- Do you both clearly understand your role in grading?
- Do you embrace multiple intelligences?
- Do students who will be evaluated using modified grading understand how their final grade will be determined?

Topics to revisit in our next meeting...

A Note from Author Lisa Dieker

At this point in the semester, evaluation and planning should be a natural part of the co-teaching process. Now is a critical time to consider if there are issues related to grading. Are all students passing the class? If all students are not being successful, what will you do to try and insure all students' success? You might want to keep John Dewey's thoughts in mind as you try to make further accommodations, "Look not for fault in the child, but in the teaching of the child."

Professional Development Resources

Murawski, W. W. & Dieker, L. A. (2004). Co-teaching at the secondary level: Unique issues, current trends, and suggestions for success. *Teaching Exceptional Children*, 36(5), 52-58.

Keefe, E. B., V. Moore, et al. (2004). The four "knows" of collaborative teaching. *Teaching Exceptional Children*, 36(5), 36-42.

TrackStar
http://trackstar.4teachers.org/

Read, Write, Think
http://www.readwritethink.org/

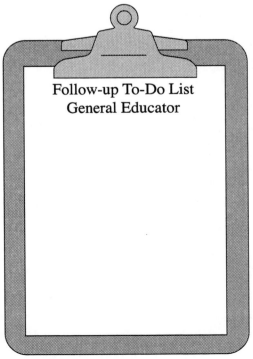

Follow-up To-Do List
General Educator

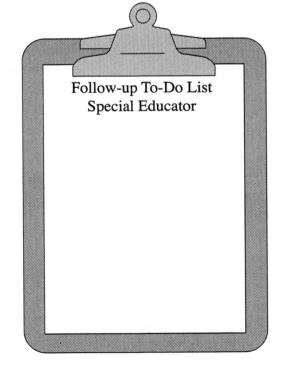

Follow-up To-Do List
Special Educator

Week of _____

Subject _____

Class Hour _____

Target Students

_____
_____
_____
_____
_____
_____

Day/Date	Big Idea/Goals	Lesson Activities	Assessment	
			Standard	Modified
Monday				
Tuesday				
Wednesday				
Thursday				
Friday				

This page is designed to be completed by the General Educator

Co-Teaching Structures:
- (O) one lead, one support
- (S) station teaching
- (P) parallel teaching
- (A) alternative teaching
- (T) team teaching

Strategy Suggestion...
Use person-first language – e.g., a person with a learning disability. If it is necessary to mention the disability, use "words with dignity."

Students with Special Needs
_____
_____
_____
_____
_____

Co-Teaching Structure	Academic Adaptations (as needed for gifted students and students with disabilities)	Behavioral Adaptations	Materials/ Support Needed	Performance Data and Notes

This page is designed to be completed by the Special Educator

Week of _____

Subject _____

Class Hour _____

Target Students
_____
_____
_____
_____
_____
_____

Day/Date	Big Idea/Goals	Lesson Activities	Assessment	
			Standard	Modified
Monday				
Tuesday				
Wednesday				
Thursday				
Friday				

This page is designed to be completed by the General Educator

Co-Teaching Structures:

(O) one lead, one support
(S) station teaching
(P) parallel teaching
(A) alternative teaching
(T) team teaching

<table>
<tr><td>Strategy Suggestion...
Concept diagrams – Student summarizes ideas within the text and organizes these ideas to illustrate a reading.</td></tr>
</table>

Students with Special Needs
_____
_____
_____
_____
_____

Co-Teaching Structure	Academic Adaptations (as needed for gifted students and students with disabilities)	Behavioral Adaptations	Materials/ Support Needed	Performance Data and Notes

This page is designed to be completed by the Special Educator

Week of _____

Subject _____

Class Hour _____

Target Students
_____
_____
_____
_____
_____

Day/Date	Big Idea/Goals	Lesson Activities	Assessment	
			Standard	Modified
Monday				
Tuesday				
Wednesday				
Thursday				
Friday				

This page is designed to be completed by the General Educator

Co-Teaching Structures:

- (O) one lead, one support
- (S) station teaching
- (P) parallel teaching
- (A) alternative teaching
- (T) team teaching

<table>
<tr><td colspan="2">Strategy Suggestion...
Test Taking –
  S - Schedule time effectively
  C - Clue words identified
  O - Omit difficult items until end
  R - Read carefully
  E - Estimate answers requiring calculations
  R - Review work and responses</td></tr>
</table>

Students with Special Needs
_____
_____
_____
_____
_____
_____

Co-Teaching Structure	Academic Adaptations (as needed for gifted students and students with disabilities)	Behavioral Adaptations	Materials/ Support Needed	Performance Data and Notes

This page is designed to be completed by the Special Educator

Week of _____

Subject _____

Class Hour _____

Target Students
_____
_____
_____
_____
_____

Day/Date	Big Idea/Goals	Lesson Activities	Assessment	
			Standard	Modified
Monday				
Tuesday				
Wednesday				
Thursday				
Friday				

This page is designed to be completed by the General Educator

Co-Teaching Structures:
- (O) one lead, one support
- (S) station teaching
- (P) parallel teaching
- (A) alternative teaching
- (T) team teaching

Students with Special Needs
_____
_____
_____
_____
_____
_____

Co-Teaching Structure	Academic Adaptations (as needed for gifted students and students with disabilities)	Behavioral Adaptations	Materials/ Support Needed	Performance Data and Notes

This page is designed to be completed by the Special Educator

Week 12 Co-Teaching Progress Check-up

Meeting Agenda
Suggested time: 30 minutes

Now is a good time to schedule a meeting between co-teaching partners to reflect on the experience to-date. Use the following agenda to guide the discussion.

1. Discuss each of the questions in the Reflective Framework (below).

2. Read and discuss the Author's Note (next page).

3. Record your thoughts and notes in the space provided for
   - Ideas
   - Topics to revisit in our next meeting
   - Follow-up to-do list for each team member

Reflective Framework

For this month's meeting, now would be a good time to review your collaborative problem solving strategies. In the problem solving process, it is critical to recognize the outside influence on any problems that arise yet identify and select solutions that are within your power to implement. Use the following discussion questions to guide the conversation:

Problem Solving (Dieker & Monda-Amaya, 1996)

- What is the problem?

- What are the issues related to the problem?

- What factors beyond the classroom may have contributed to the problem?

- What solutions could be used to solve the problem?

- What can we do to solve the problem?

- What justification can we provide to support our solution(s)?

Topics to revisit in our next meeting...

A Note from Author Lisa Dieker

On the opposite page I have provided a problem-solving framework to use during your team planning time. A natural part of any teaming process involves dealing with problems. The questions were derived from observing effective teachers solve problems related to students with disabilities. Success is dependent on taking ownership and action to resolve any problems as they arise.

One issue many teams fail to discuss until the end of the semester is grading. Now is the time to adjust grading criteria, if necessary, for all students.

Professional Development Resources

Laframboise, K. L., Epanchin, B., et al. (2004). Working together: Emerging roles of special and general education teachers in inclusive settings. *Action in Teacher Education,* 26(3), 29-43.

Dukes, C. (2006) Special education: An integral part of small schools in high schools. *The High School Journal,* 89(3), 1-9.

Dave's ESL Cafe
http://www.eslcafe.com/

Spark Notes
http://www.sparknotes.com/

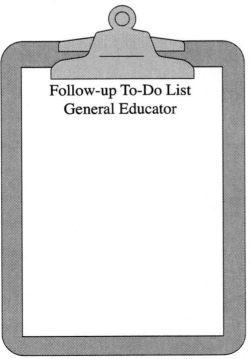

Follow-up To-Do List
General Educator

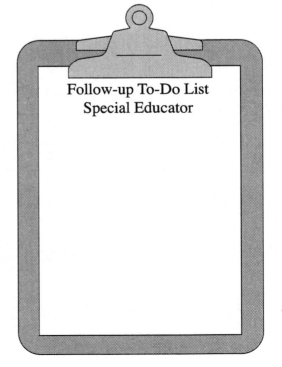

Follow-up To-Do List
Special Educator

Week of _____

Subject _____

Class Hour _____

Target Students
_____
_____
_____
_____
_____

Day/Date	Big Idea/Goals	Lesson Activities	Assessment	
			Standard	Modified
Monday				
Tuesday				
Wednesday				
Thursday				
Friday				

This page is designed to be completed by the General Educator

Co-Teaching Structures:
- (O) one lead, one support
- (S) station teaching
- (P) parallel teaching
- (A) alternative teaching
- (T) team teaching

Strategy Suggestion...
PURPOSE – a structured teaching model:
P - Prepare the student to learn the skill
U - Understand and learn the skill steps
R - Rehearse the skill correctly
P - Perform a self-check on the skill
O - Overcome any skill performance problems
S - Other situations the skill can be used
E - Evaluate skill performance

Students with Special Needs
_____
_____
_____
_____
_____
_____

Co-Teaching Structure	Academic Adaptations (as needed for gifted students and students with disabilities)	Behavioral Adaptations	Materials/ Support Needed	Performance Data and Notes

This page is designed to be completed by the Special Educator

Week of _____

Subject _____

Class Hour _____

Target Students
_____
_____
_____
_____
_____

Day/Date	Big Idea/Goals	Lesson Activities	Assessment	
			Standard	Modified
Monday				
Tuesday				
Wednesday				
Thursday				
Friday				

This page is designed to be completed by the General Educator

Co-Teaching Structures:

(O) one lead, one support
(S) station teaching
(P) parallel teaching
(A) alternative teaching
(T) team teaching

Strategy Suggestion...
Visual imagery – Have students create and share mental images from a story.

Students with Special Needs
_____
_____
_____
_____
_____

Co-Teaching Structure	Academic Adaptations (as needed for gifted students and students with disabilities)	Behavioral Adaptations	Materials/ Support Needed	Performance Data and Notes

This page is designed to be completed by the Special Educator

Week of _____

Subject _____

Class Hour _____

Strategy Suggestion...
Prereading techniques – Set a purpose, preview vocabulary, activate background knowledge, and relate background knowledge to new knowledge.

Target Students
_____
_____
_____
_____
_____

Day/Date	Big Idea/Goals	Lesson Activities	Assessment	
			Standard	Modified
Monday				
Tuesday				
Wednesday				
Thursday				
Friday				

This page is designed to be completed by the General Educator

Co-Teaching Structures:

(O) one lead, one support
(S) station teaching
(P) parallel teaching
(A) alternative teaching
(T) team teaching

Students with Special Needs
_____
_____
_____
_____
_____

Co-Teaching Structure	Academic Adaptations (as needed for gifted students and students with disabilities)	Behavioral Adaptations	Materials/ Support Needed	Performance Data and Notes

This page is designed to be completed by the Special Educator

Week of _____

Subject _____

Class Hour _____

Target Students
_____
_____
_____
_____
_____
_____

Day/Date	Big Idea/Goals	Lesson Activities	Assessment	
			Standard	Modified
Monday				
Tuesday				
Wednesday				
Thursday				
Friday				

This page is designed to be completed by the General Educator

Co-Teaching Structures:

- (O) one lead, one support
- (S) station teaching
- (P) parallel teaching
- (A) alternative teaching
- (T) team teaching

Students with Special Needs

_____
_____
_____
_____
_____

Co-Teaching Structure	Academic Adaptations (as needed for gifted students and students with disabilities)	Behavioral Adaptations	Materials/ Support Needed	Performance Data and Notes

This page is designed to be completed by the Special Educator

Week 16 Co-Teaching Progress Check-up

Meeting Agenda
Suggested time: 30 minutes

Now is a good time to schedule a meeting between co-teaching partners to reflect on the experience to-date. Use the following agenda to guide the discussion.

Ideas

1. Discuss each of the questions in the Reflective Framework (below).

2. Read and discuss the Author's Note (next page).

3. Record your thoughts and notes in the space provided for
   - Ideas
   - Topics to revisit in our next meeting
   - Follow-up to-do list for each team member

Reflective Framework

As the semester draws to a close, now would be a good time to carefully consider the success individual students have achieved this semester. As well as the success you have had in coteaching. Rarely do students or others thank us but you can both thank each other for the amazing impact you have on children's lives. After sharing your appreciation, use the following discussion questions to guide the conversation:

Evaluation (Dieker, 2006)

- Did we meet the needs of all students this semester?

- Were there academic tasks/behaviors that we found difficult to deal with this semester?

- Are there issues in which we need support in order to successfully meet the needs of all students?

- Are there other students in which it would be beneficial for us to discuss how to effectively meet their needs?

Topics to revisit in our next meeting...

A Note from Author Lisa Dieker

Now is the time to assess the current co-taught classroom and to begin planning any needed changes for next semester. Here are some specific topics you may want to discuss:

- roles for each team member
- administrator involvement
- class composition
- grading
- ensuring IEPs for all students are being addressed
- additional resources needed

Professional Development Resources

Luckner, J. (199). An examination of two coteaching classrooms. *American Annals of the Deaf*, 144(1), 24-34.

Murawski, W. (2005). Addressing diverse needs through co-teaching. *Kappa Delta Pi*, 41(2), 77-82.

BookShare.Org
http://www.bookshare.org/

Cool Site of the Day
http://cool.infi.net/

Follow-up To-Do List
General Educator

Follow-up To-Do List
Special Educator

Week of _____

Subject _____

Class Hour _____

Target Students
_____
_____
_____
_____
_____

Day/Date	Big Idea/Goals	Lesson Activities	Assessment	
			Standard	Modified
Monday				
Tuesday				
Wednesday				
Thursday				
Friday				

This page is designed to be completed by the General Educator

Co-Teaching Structures:

(O) one lead, one support
(S) station teaching
(P) parallel teaching
(A) alternative teaching
(T) team teaching

Strategy Suggestion...

Spirit reading – A student continues to read until the "spirit moves" them to stop and then any other student who the "spirit moves" can start reading.

Students with Special Needs
_____
_____
_____
_____
_____

Co-Teaching Structure	Academic Adaptations (as needed for gifted students and students with disabilities)	Behavioral Adaptations	Materials/ Support Needed	Performance Data and Notes

This page is designed to be completed by the Special Educator

Week of _____

Subject _____

Class Hour _____

Strategy Suggestion...
Readability issues – When a text is just too difficult: provide the same content at an easier level, provide assistance with an organizer or study guide, or offer alternative formats (e.g., video, audio tape, pictures, computer).

Target Students
_____
_____
_____
_____
_____
_____

Day/Date	Big Idea/Goals	Lesson Activities	Assessment	
			Standard	Modified
Monday				
Tuesday				
Wednesday				
Thursday				
Friday				

This page is designed to be completed by the General Educator

Co-Teaching Structures:

(O) one lead, one support
(S) station teaching
(P) parallel teaching
(A) alternative teaching
(T) team teaching

Strategy Suggestion...

Summary mark-out – As students read a passage, have them mark out non-critical information (go over the passage 2-3 times). Summarize the remaining information in 10 words or less to represent the main idea of the passage.

Students with Special Needs

_____
_____
_____
_____
_____
_____

Co-Teaching Structure	Academic Adaptations (as needed for gifted students and students with disabilities)	Behavioral Adaptations	Materials/ Support Needed	Performance Data and Notes

This page is designed to be completed by the Special Educator

Week of _____

Subject _____

Class Hour _____

Target Students
_____
_____
_____
_____
_____

Day/Date	Big Idea/Goals	Lesson Activities	Assessment	
			Standard	Modified
Monday				
Tuesday				
Wednesday				
Thursday				
Friday				

This page is designed to be completed by the General Educator

Co-Teaching Structures:
- (O) one lead, one support
- (S) station teaching
- (P) parallel teaching
- (A) alternative teaching
- (T) team teaching

Strategy Suggestion...
Create a CD cover – Have students create a CD cover with song titles that reflect the key ideas in a chapter or story they have read.

Students with Special Needs
_____
_____
_____
_____
_____

Co-Teaching Structure	Academic Adaptations (as needed for gifted students and students with disabilities)	Behavioral Adaptations	Materials/ Support Needed	Performance Data and Notes

This page is designed to be completed by the Special Educator

Week of _____

Subject _____

Class Hour _____

Target Students

_____
_____
_____
_____
_____

Day/Date	Big Idea/Goals	Lesson Activities	Assessment	
			Standard	Modified
Monday				
Tuesday				
Wednesday				
Thursday				
Friday				

This page is designed to be completed by the General Educator

INCLUSION RESOURCES
featuring Lisa Dieker, Ph.D.

BOOK

The Co-Teaching Lesson Plan Book, 3rd Ed.

This unique lesson plan book is designed to be completed and shared by a general education teacher and a special education teacher.

Revised and updated to gather evidence of academic and behavioral adaptations as required by IDEA. Planning tools for standard and modified assessment will facilitate efforts to monitor student performance and achievement of NCLB goals.

Includes weekly strategies and monthly notes from the author that offer insight about the value, the art, and the impact of co-teaching.

2006, spiral bound, 110 pages
Order # CTLP-LPB
$19.95

Winning Strategies for Inclusive Classrooms (Elementary)

Dr. Rebecca Hines, &
Dr. Lisa Dieker, Ph.D.

From two of the most dynamic teacher trainers in the country, comes an exciting and powerful program that addresses:

- Effective Co-Teaching
- Time & Management Strategies
- The Skilled Use of Paraeducators
- Co-Teaching Roles & Responsibilities
- Teamwork & Collaboration

Also included is a ***Viewer's Guide*** to assist staff developers, trainers and coaches in building successful Inclusion/Co-Teaching teams!

2009, DVD, Closed-captioned, 40 minutes
Order # DWSI-LPB $139.95

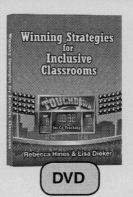

DVD

---

7 Effective Strategies for Secondary Inclusion

Inclusion of students with disabilities is never an easy task! It is especially challenging in secondary schools where departmentalization and the focus on high stakes testing can present significant obstacles. Learn about:

- Creating a school-wide culture
- Celebrating success for all students
- Developing interdisciplinary collaboration
- Implementing effective co-teaching
- Establishing active learning
- Improving grading & student assessments
- Implementing effective instruction

DVD, 2006, 65 minutes   Order # D7ES-LPB $129.95

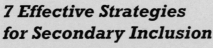

DVD

BOOK

Demystifying Secondary Inclusion: **Powerful Schoolwide & Classroom Strategies**

This book expands on the content presented by **Lisa Dieker** in her DVD, *7 Effective Strategies for Secondary Inclusion*. Dr. Dieker focuses both on schoolwide, as well as "universally designed" classroom-based approaches. She provides practical solutions to implement inclusion by addressing the many challenges presented by students and teachers in secondary learning environments. The theme is that "together we are better," and our collaborative efforts must listen to the most important voices—that of our students.

2006, soft cover, 194 pages
Order # DSIP-LPB $29.95

See last page for ORDER FORM

Visit www.NPRinc.com for more great resources!

MEMO

To: Building Principal
        Director of Special Education

From: _____

RE: Co-Teaching Lesson Plan Book Reorder

On the back side of this memo, please find a completed order form for ordering new copies of The Co-Teaching Lesson Plan Book for next school year.

Please process this order as soon as possible so that we may have the plan books available for our co-teaching efforts next year.

Co-Teaching Structures:

(O) one lead, one support
(S) station teaching
(P) parallel teaching
(A) alternative teaching
(T) team teaching

	Strategy Suggestion...
	Commercials – Have students write and videotape a commercial related to a book they have read.

Students with Special Needs
_____
_____
_____
_____
_____
_____

Co-Teaching Structure	Academic Adaptations (as needed for gifted students and students with disabilities)	Behavioral Adaptations	Materials/ Support Needed	Performance Data and Notes

This page is designed to be completed by the Special Educator

Week 20 Co-Teaching Progress Check-up

Meeting Agenda
Suggested time: 30 minutes

Now is a good time to schedule a meeting between co-teaching partners to reflect on the experience to-date. Use the following agenda to guide the discussion.

1. Discuss each of the questions in the Reflective Framework (below).

2. Read and discuss the Author's Note (next page).

3. Record your thoughts and notes in the space provided for
   - Ideas
   - Topics to revisit in our next meeting
   - Follow-up to-do list for each team member

Reflective Framework

As you reflect on the accommodations you have made, you may want to keep the following guidelines in mind:

• Have you shared the accommodations with parents so they can be reinforced at home?

• Are both general and special education teachers generating ideas?

• Are students asked to assess the value of the accommodations?

• Are the accommodations related to classroom tasks and the general education curriculum?

• Are these accommodations reasonable and still meet the needs of all students?

• Are these accommodations empowering rather than humiliating?

• Do students with disabilities have the opportunity to give as well as receive in your class?

Topics to revisit in our next meeting...

A Note from Author Lisa Dieker

At this point in the school year you may want to do a health checkup on your relationship as well as the accommodations being provided to students with disabilities. As the year progresses, it is critical to consider if you are providing each other with positive and productive energy in your relationship. For students, now is an excellent time to consider if accommodations are allowing enough independence and skills to prepare them for the next grade level.

Professional Development Resources

Weiss, M. P., & Lloyd, J. (2003). Conditions for Co-teaching: Lessons from a case study. *Teacher Education and Special Education*, 26(1), 27-41.

Shriner, J., & Destefano, L. (2003). Participation and accommodation in state assessment: The role of individualized education programs. *Exceptional Children*, 69, 147-161.

Windows on the Universe
http://www.windows.ucar.edu/

News-2-You
http://www.news-2-you.com/

Follow-up To-Do List
General Educator

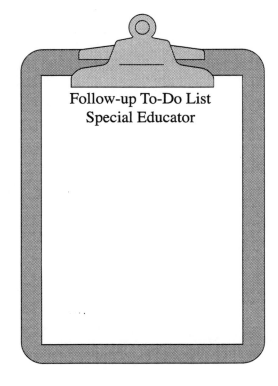

Follow-up To-Do List
Special Educator

Week of _____

Subject _____

Class Hour _____

Target Students
_____
_____
_____
_____
_____

Day/Date	Big Idea/Goals	Lesson Activities	Assessment	
			Standard	Modified
Monday				
Tuesday				
Wednesday				
Thursday				
Friday				

This page is designed to be completed by the General Educator

Co-Teaching Structures:

(O) one lead, one support
(S) station teaching
(P) parallel teaching
(A) alternative teaching
(T) team teaching

<table>
<tr><td>Strategy Suggestion...
Develop a timeline – Ask students to develop a timeline of the events that occurred in a story or across several chapters.</td></tr>
</table>

Students with Special Needs
_____
_____
_____
_____
_____
_____

Co-Teaching Structure	Academic Adaptations (as needed for gifted students and students with disabilities)	Behavioral Adaptations	Materials/ Support Needed	Performance Data and Notes

This page is designed to be completed by the Special Educator

Week of _____

Subject _____

Class Hour _____

Target Students
_____
_____
_____
_____
_____
_____

Day/Date	Big Idea/Goals	Lesson Activities	Assessment	
			Standard	Modified
Monday				
Tuesday				
Wednesday				
Thursday				
Friday				

This page is designed to be completed by the General Educator

Co-Teaching Structures:
- (O) one lead, one support
- (S) station teaching
- (P) parallel teaching
- (A) alternative teaching
- (T) team teaching

Strategy Suggestion...
KWL
K = What you already Know
W = What you Want to know
L = What you Learned

Students with Special Needs
_____
_____
_____
_____
_____

Co-Teaching Structure	Academic Adaptations (as needed for gifted students and students with disabilities)	Behavioral Adaptations	Materials/ Support Needed	Performance Data and Notes

This page is designed to be completed by the Special Educator

Week of _____

Subject _____

Class Hour _____

Strategy Suggestion...
Popcorn – Students read aloud and can say "popcorn" followed by the name of a peer in order to change readers.

Target Students

_____
_____
_____
_____
_____

Day/Date	Big Idea/Goals	Lesson Activities	Assessment	
			Standard	Modified
Monday				
Tuesday				
Wednesday				
Thursday				
Friday				

This page is designed to be completed by the General Educator

Co-Teaching Structures:

(O) one lead, one support
(S) station teaching
(P) parallel teaching
(A) alternative teaching
(T) team teaching

Strategy Suggestion...

Five finger rule – When students are selecting a book to read, share this rule: If in reading the first few pages, you know all the words except five, and can ask yourself and answer five questions about what you have read, then this is probably a good book for you.

Students with Special Needs
_____
_____
_____
_____
_____
_____

Co-Teaching Structure	Academic Adaptations (as needed for gifted students and students with disabilities)	Behavioral Adaptations	Materials/ Support Needed	Performance Data and Notes

This page is designed to be completed by the Special Educator

Week of _____

Subject _____

Class Hour _____

Target Students
_____
_____
_____
_____
_____

Day/Date	Big Idea/Goals	Lesson Activities	Assessment	
			Standard	Modified
Monday				
Tuesday				
Wednesday				
Thursday				
Friday				

This page is designed to be completed by the General Educator

Co-Teaching Structures:

(O) one lead, one support
(S) station teaching
(P) parallel teaching
(A) alternative teaching
(T) team teaching

Strategy Suggestion...

Pass a sentence – With cooperative groups, write a starter sentence, pass the sentence to each student asking each to contribute a sentence until the group generates a paragraph.

Students with Special Needs

_____
_____
_____
_____
_____

Co-Teaching Structure	Academic Adaptations (as needed for gifted students and students with disabilities)	Behavioral Adaptations	Materials/ Support Needed	Performance Data and Notes

This page is designed to be completed by the Special Educator

Week 24 Co-Teaching Progress Check-up

Meeting Agenda
Suggested time: 30 minutes

Now is a good time to schedule a meeting between co-teaching partners to reflect on the experience to-date. Use the following agenda to guide the discussion.

1. Discuss each of the questions in the Reflective Framework (below).

2. Read and discuss the Author's Note (next page).

3. Record your thoughts and notes in the space provided for
   - Ideas
   - Topics to revisit in our next meeting
   - Follow-up to-do list for each team member

Reflective Framework

Consider developing a matrix like the one below. The first column contains the IEP goals for a caseload of students. Across the top of the other columns are the names of the individual students. The dots illustrate that a specific goal is on the student's IEP and needs to be monitored in the co-taught setting. This type of matrix can be used by co-teachers to monitor students' progress toward goals and help focus planning for students' individual learning or behavior needs.

	Tom	Jim	Bill	Sue
Respects others and property	•			
Positive attitude/behavior related to teachers, peers	•	•		
Completes and submits homework as assigned	•		•	•
Brings and completes assignment book daily	•		•	•
Breaks down tasks and completes on time				•

Topics to revisit in our next meeting...

A Note from Author Lisa Dieker

How are you gathering data on IEP progress? I believe students with disabilities should be given credit for the two curriculua (the general education curriculum and their IEPs) they are expected to master. Too many times students are only evaluated on the general education curriculum. Yet they are not successful in the general education curriculum because of what's on their IEPs. Therefore, be certain you are teaching to both and evaluating both areas.

Professional Development Resources

Dieker, L. A., & Murawski, W. W. (2003). Co-teaching at the secondary level: Unique issues, current trends, and suggestions for success. *The High School Journal*, 86 (4), 1-13.

Austin, V. L. (2001). Teacher's beliefs about co-teaching. *Remedial and Special Education*, 22(4), 245-255.

SparkTop
http://www.sparktop.org/

Wikipedia
http://en.wikipedia.org/

Follow-up To-Do List
General Educator

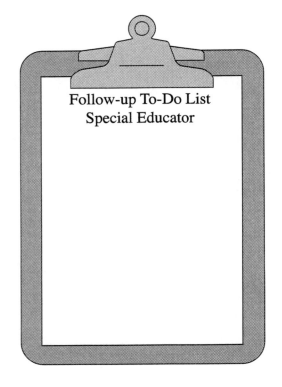

Follow-up To-Do List
Special Educator

Week of _____

Subject _____

Class Hour _____

<table>
<tr><td>Strategy Suggestion...
Interviews – Have students write interview questions. Answer the questions as you explore various topics.</td></tr>
</table>

Day/Date	Big Idea/Goals	Lesson Activities	Assessment	
			Standard	Modified
Monday				
Tuesday				
Wednesday				
Thursday				
Friday				

This page is designed to be completed by the General Educator

Co-Teaching Structures:

- (O) one lead, one support
- (S) station teaching
- (P) parallel teaching
- (A) alternative teaching
- (T) team teaching

Strategy Suggestion...
Vocabulary book: In each subject, have students keep a vocabulary book of words they are struggling to learn. Allow some students to add pictures to help them remember the defintions.

Students with Special Needs
_____
_____
_____
_____
_____

Co-Teaching Structure	Academic Adaptations (as needed for gifted students and students with disabilities)	Behavioral Adaptations	Materials/ Support Needed	Performance Data and Notes

This page is designed to be completed by the Special Educator

Week of _____

Subject _____

Class Hour _____

Target Students
_____
_____
_____
_____
_____
_____

Day/Date	Big Idea/Goals	Lesson Activities	Assessment	
			Standard	Modified
Monday				
Tuesday				
Wednesday				
Thursday				
Friday				

This page is designed to be completed by the General Educator

Co-Teaching Structures:

- (O) one lead, one support
- (S) station teaching
- (P) parallel teaching
- (A) alternative teaching
- (T) team teaching

Strategy Suggestion...
Teach students how to use the textbook – Help students use visual aids, find definitions to vocabulary, and how to identify the important points.

Students with Special Needs
_____
_____
_____
_____
_____

Co-Teaching Structure	Academic Adaptations (as needed for gifted students and students with disabilities)	Behavioral Adaptations	Materials/ Support Needed	Performance Data and Notes

This page is designed to be completed by the Special Educator

Week of _____

Subject _____

Class Hour _____

Target Students

_____
_____
_____
_____
_____

Day/Date	Big Idea/Goals	Lesson Activities	Assessment	
			Standard	Modified
Monday				
Tuesday				
Wednesday				
Thursday				
Friday				

This page is designed to be completed by the General Educator

Co-Teaching Structures:

(O) one lead, one support
(S) station teaching
(P) parallel teaching
(A) alternative teaching
(T) team teaching

Strategy Suggestion...
Turned paper – Turn notebook paper sideways to use lines for math problems. Provide answers or fill-in-the-blank questions.

Students with Special Needs
_____
_____
_____
_____
_____

Co-Teaching Structure	Academic Adaptations (as needed for gifted students and students with disabilities)	Behavioral Adaptations	Materials/ Support Needed	Performance Data and Notes

This page is designed to be completed by the Special Educator

		Strategy Suggestion...	Target Students

Week of _____

Subject _____

Class Hour _____

Strategy Suggestion...
Simplify the process – Simplify directions for seatwork by verbally presenting them, writing alternative sets of directions, highlighting important words in directions, or have students help each other.

Target Students
_____
_____
_____
_____
_____

Day/Date	Big Idea/Goals	Lesson Activities	Assessment	
			Standard	Modified
Monday				
Tuesday				
Wednesday				
Thursday				
Friday				

This page is designed to be completed by the General Educator

Co-Teaching Structures:

(O) one lead, one support
(S) station teaching
(P) parallel teaching
(A) alternative teaching
(T) team teaching

Strategy Suggestion...
Expectations: State your academic and behavioral expectations at the beginning of each class.

Students with Special Needs
_____
_____
_____
_____
_____

Co-Teaching Structure	Academic Adaptations (as needed for gifted students and students with disabilities)	Behavioral Adaptations	Materials/ Support Needed	Performance Data and Notes

This page is designed to be completed by the Special Educator

Week 28 Co-Teaching Progress Check-up

Meeting Agenda
Suggested time: 30 minutes

Now is a good time to schedule a meeting between co-teaching partners to reflect on the experience to-date. Use the following agenda to guide the discussion.

Ideas

1. Discuss each of the questions in the Reflective Framework (below).

2. Read and discuss the Author's Note (next page).

3. Record your thoughts and notes in the space provided for
   - Ideas
   - Topics to revisit in our next meeting
   - Follow-up to-do list for each team member

Reflective Framework

Colleague Janet Hill has given me permission to summarize some of her key ideas for supporting students before/during/after testing. Try them out with your students!

Before the Test
- Create and use concept maps, study guides, and graphic organizers
- Prepare note cards
- Determine test modifications
- Take practice tests
- Hold individual and group review sessions
- Practice test taking strategies

During the Test
- Check everyone's anxiety level
- Give immediate feedback
- Complete one problem/question in every section
- Request teacher assistance as needed
- Complete test at alternate site if necessary
- Practice self monitoring
- Utilize extended time (if provided)

After the Test
- Retake all or part of the test (if permittable)
- Make corrections on incorrect problems
- Consider alternative grading approaches such as partial credit, grade only a subset of questions, etc.

Topics to revisit in our next meeting...

A Note from Author Lisa Dieker

Brain research informs us that learning and memory is greatly impacted by anxiety. This month I have provided you with some tips from a colleague to assist with testing.

Keep in mind that a discussion related to state proficiency testing should be a core part of the planning and the accommodations discussed for students with disabilities. Remember, students must be taught how to use their accommodations prior to state testing so make teaching these skills part of your planning.

Professional Development Resources

Wischnowski, M. W., Salmon, S. J., & Eaton, K. (2004, Summer). Evaluating co-teaching as a means for successful inclusion of students with disabilities in a rural district. *Rural Special Education Quarterly*, 18(1), 5-11.

Dieker, L., & Little, M (2005). Secondary reading: Not just for reading teachers anymore. *Intervention in School and Clinic*, 40, 276-283.

Closing the Gap
http://www.closingthegap.com

AT Training Online
http://atto.buffalo.edu/

Follow-up To-Do List
General Educator

Follow-up To-Do List
Special Educator

Week of _____

Subject _____

Class Hour _____

Target Students

_____
_____
_____
_____
_____

Day/Date	Big Idea/Goals	Lesson Activities	Assessment	
			Standard	Modified
Monday				
Tuesday				
Wednesday				
Thursday				
Friday				

This page is designed to be completed by the General Educator

Co-Teaching Structures:

- (O) one lead, one support
- (S) station teaching
- (P) parallel teaching
- (A) alternative teaching
- (T) team teaching

Students with Special Needs

_____
_____
_____
_____
_____
_____

Co-Teaching Structure	Academic Adaptations (as needed for gifted students and students with disabilities)	Behavioral Adaptations	Materials/ Support Needed	Performance Data and Notes

This page is designed to be completed by the Special Educator

Week of _____

Subject _____

Class Hour _____

Target Students
_____
_____
_____
_____
_____
_____

Day/Date	Big Idea/Goals	Lesson Activities	Assessment	
			Standard	Modified
Monday				
Tuesday				
Wednesday				
Thursday				
Friday				

This page is designed to be completed by the General Educator

Co-Teaching Structures:
- (O) one lead, one support
- (S) station teaching
- (P) parallel teaching
- (A) alternative teaching
- (T) team teaching

Strategy Suggestion...
Individualized homework – Give students opportunities to develop their own homework after offering examples.

Students with Special Needs
_____
_____
_____
_____
_____

Co-Teaching Structure	Academic Adaptations (as needed for gifted students and students with disabilities)	Behavioral Adaptations	Materials/ Support Needed	Performance Data and Notes

This page is designed to be completed by the Special Educator

Week of _____

Subject _____

Class Hour _____

Target Students

_____
_____
_____
_____
_____

Day/Date	Big Idea/Goals	Lesson Activities	Assessment	
			Standard	Modified
Monday				
Tuesday				
Wednesday				
Thursday				
Friday				

This page is designed to be completed by the General Educator

Co-Teaching Structures:
(O) one lead, one support
(S) station teaching
(P) parallel teaching
(A) alternative teaching
(T) team teaching

Strategy Suggestion...
Assure student access – Ask your occupational or physical therapist to review the accessibility of your lab space and instructional materials.

Students with Special Needs
_____
_____
_____
_____
_____

Co-Teaching Structure	Academic Adaptations (as needed for gifted students and students with disabilities)	Behavioral Adaptations	Materials/ Support Needed	Performance Data and Notes

This page is designed to be completed by the Special Educator

Week of _____

Subject _____

Class Hour _____

Target Students
_____
_____
_____
_____
_____
_____

Day/Date	Big Idea/Goals	Lesson Activities	Assessment	
			Standard	Modified
Monday				
Tuesday				
Wednesday				
Thursday				
Friday				

This page is designed to be completed by the General Educator

Co-Teaching Structures:

(O) one lead, one support
(S) station teaching
(P) parallel teaching
(A) alternative teaching
(T) team teaching

Strategy Suggestion...
Alternative lessons outcomes –
Allow students to demonstrate under-
standing of a concept at a different
level or in a different format.

Students with Special Needs

_____
_____
_____
_____
_____

Co-Teaching Structure	Academic Adaptations (as needed for gifted students and students with disabilities)	Behavioral Adaptations	Materials/ Support Needed	Performance Data and Notes

This page is designed to be completed by the Special Educator

Week 32 Co-Teaching Progress Check-up

Meeting Agenda
Suggested time: 30 minutes

Now is a good time to schedule a meeting between co-teaching partners to reflect on the experience to-date. Use the following agenda to guide the discussion.

1. Discuss each of the questions in the Reflective Framework (below).

2. Read and discuss the Author's Note (next page).

3. Record your thoughts and notes in the space provided for
   - Ideas
   - Topics to revisit in our next meeting
   - Follow-up to-do list for each team member

Ideas

Reflective Framework

As the end of the year approaches, now is a good time to do a mental health check-up. Discuss the following questions:

• Are you ending the year with a list of 10 positive things you accomplished?

• Can you list 5 or more reasons as to why you should co-teach again next year?

• Have you shared with administrators how you would like your co-teaching schedule to be structured for next year?

• What 1-2 things will you focus on improving in your co-teaching relationship(s) next year?

• What is the nicest thing you will do for yourselves over the summer?

• Have you ordered a new co-teaching plan book for next year?

Topics to revisit in our next meeting...

*A Note from Author
Lisa Dieker*

The last few weeks of the school year always present mixed feelings of anticipation for summer and a need to be sure all students are ready for the next grade level. In the weeks remaining, how can you strategically plan to ensure they are ready?

To help put a positive spin on the daily chore of teaching, go out of your way to affirm all your colleagues, and especially your co-teaching peer. If you are tired, you should be! Research shows as a teacher you make over 1,300 decisions a day. Use these decisions wisely and stay positive!

Professional Development Resources

Walsh, J. M., & Jones, B. (2004). New models of cooperative teaching. *Teaching Exceptional Children*, 36(5),14-20.

Weiss, M.P. (2004). Co-teaching as science in the schoolhouse: More questions than answers. *Journal of Learning Disabilities*, 37(3), 218-223.

4Teachers
http://www.4teachers.org/

Busy Teachers' Web Site
http://www.ceismc.gatech.edu/busyt/

Follow-up To-Do List
General Educator

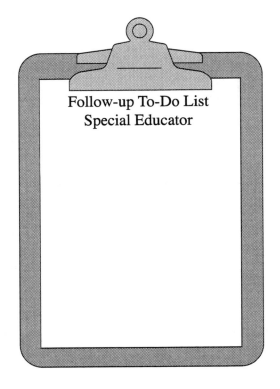

Follow-up To-Do List
Special Educator

Week of _____

Subject _____

Class Hour _____

Target Students

_____
_____
_____
_____
_____

Day/Date	Big Idea/Goals	Lesson Activities	Assessment	
			Standard	Modified
Monday				
Tuesday				
Wednesday				
Thursday				
Friday				

This page is designed to be completed by the General Educator

Co-Teaching Structures:

- (O) one lead, one support
- (S) station teaching
- (P) parallel teaching
- (A) alternative teaching
- (T) team teaching

<table>
<tr><td colspan="2">*Strategy Suggestion...*</td></tr>
<tr><td colspan="2">Directions – Since many directions involve multiple steps, consider: providing some students with only one step at a time; ask students to repeat the directions they heard in their own words; or alternate talking and demonstrating.</td></tr>
</table>

Students with Special Needs
_____
_____
_____
_____
_____

Co-Teaching Structure	Academic Adaptations (as needed for gifted students and students with disabilities)	Behavioral Adaptations	Materials/ Support Needed	Performance Data and Notes

This page is designed to be completed by the Special Educator

Week of _____

Subject _____

Class Hour _____

Target Students
_____
_____
_____
_____
_____

Day/Date	Big Idea/Goals	Lesson Activities	Assessment	
			Standard	Modified
Monday				
Tuesday				
Wednesday				
Thursday				
Friday				

This page is designed to be completed by the General Educator

Co-Teaching Structures:

- (O) one lead, one support
- (S) station teaching
- (P) parallel teaching
- (A) alternative teaching
- (T) team teaching

Strategy Suggestion...

Share findings with other students – Remember to prepare a group for the accommodations needed by a student who has hearing or vision impairments. For a student with behavioral issues, give them a role that is not overwhelming and is likely to ensure success with their peers.

Students with Special Needs

_____

_____

_____

_____

_____

Co-Teaching Structure	Academic Adaptations (as needed for gifted students and students with disabilities)	Behavioral Adaptations	Materials/ Support Needed	Performance Data and Notes

This page is designed to be completed by the Special Educator

Week of _____
Subject _____
Class Hour _____

Strategy Suggestion...
Consider alternative outcomes – Participation, observation, or appreciation could be used to evaluate student outcomes in some subject areas.

Target Students
_____
_____
_____
_____
_____
_____

Day/Date	Big Idea/Goals	Lesson Activities	Assessment	
			Standard	Modified
Monday				
Tuesday				
Wednesday				
Thursday				
Friday				

This page is designed to be completed by the General Educator

Co-Teaching Structures:

- (O) one lead, one support
- (S) station teaching
- (P) parallel teaching
- (A) alternative teaching
- (T) team teaching

Strategy Suggestion...

Create a checklist – Make a list of the major skills for each quarter and ask the student or a special educator to help assess what skills a student can or cannot easily accomplish.

Students with Special Needs

_____

_____

_____

_____

_____

Co-Teaching Structure	Academic Adaptations (as needed for gifted students and students with disabilities)	Behavioral Adaptations	Materials/ Support Needed	Performance Data and Notes

This page is designed to be completed by the Special Educator

Week of _____

Subject _____

Class Hour _____

Strategy Suggestion...
Coordinate your material with content area material – Consider how you can reinforce all the subject areas that students experience each day (e.g., use words from P.E. in your writing assignments). All students will learn more effectively when subject areas are connected.

Target Students
_____
_____
_____
_____
_____

Day/Date	Big Idea/Goals	Lesson Activities	Assessment	
			Standard	Modified
Monday				
Tuesday				
Wednesday				
Thursday				
Friday				

This page is designed to be completed by the General Educator

Co-Teaching Structures:
- (O) one lead, one support
- (S) station teaching
- (P) parallel teaching
- (A) alternative teaching
- (T) team teaching

<table>
<tr><td colspan="3">Strategy Suggestion...
Reduce the number of materials –
Often, less is more. Give students
only two choices instead of the numerous choices given in some subject areas.</td></tr>
</table>

Students with Special Needs
_____
_____
_____
_____

Co-Teaching Structure	Academic Adaptations (as needed for gifted students and students with disabilities)	Behavioral Adaptations	Materials/ Support Needed	Performance Data and Notes

This page is designed to be completed by the Special Educator

Week 36 Co-Teaching Progress Check-up

Meeting Agenda
Suggested time: 30 minutes

Now is a good time to schedule a meeting between co-teaching partners to reflect on the experience to-date. Use the following agenda to guide the discussion.

1. Discuss each of the questions in the Reflective Framework (below).

2. Read and discuss the Author's Note (next page).

3. Record your thoughts and notes in the space provided for
   - Ideas
   - Topics to revisit in our next meeting
   - Follow-up to-do list for each team member

Ideas

Reflective Framework

As the school year draws to a close, now would be a good time to carefully consider the success individual students have achieved this past year. Use the following discussion questions to guide the conversation:

- How do you both feel about your roles as co-teachers?

- Are there changes you need to make before the start of next year?

- Are there other support staff you need to have involved in ensuring the success of all students (e.g., administrator, social worker, guidance counselor)?

- Have you clearly discussed the curricular expectations for the next year as well as the IEP needs of students in the class?

- Will there be state or proficiency testing that will occur next fall? If so, how have you prepared the students and will there be modifications made for the students with disabilities?

- Have you both shared something positive about your co-teaching relationship with each other, a colleague, and an administrator?

- What are the best things you plan to do over the summer break?

A Note from Author
Lisa Dieker

Congratulations on completing what I hope was a successful and rewarding co-teaching year. Co-teaching is a powerful tool to allow students with disabilities to be included in the general education setting.

If this is your first year co-teaching, I encourage you to continue to expand upon this opportunity across grade levels and content areas for your own professional growth and to meet the needs of all students. If you are a veteran team, now is a great time to reflect on the strength of your team and what challenges you might address to make your team even more successful. Never forget the primary goal of your lesson every day is to meet the needs of each and every child.

As you continue to move forward, please remember that change in schools comes slowly. It doesn't matter how slowly you go, as long as you do not stop!

Follow-up To-Do List
General Educator

Follow-up To-Do List
Special Educator

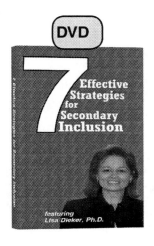

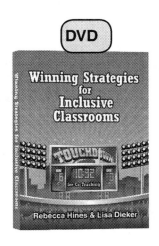

BOOK

Visit www.NPRinc.com for more detailed descriptions and *BEST SELLING* resources!

✱SPECIAL OFFER: Order 20 or more *Co-Teaching Lesson Plan Books* and receive a 50% discount off of either of the above listed DVDs or book! Call 1-800-453-7461 to place your order.

ORDER FORM

SHIP TO:

Name

School/Institution

Street Address

City   State   Zip Code

( )

Daytime Phone

PAYMENT METHOD:

☐ Check enclosed payable to National Professional Resources, Inc.

☐ Purchase Order Number _____

☐ Visa   ☐ MasterCard   ☐ AmEx

Card Number   Exp. Date

Name on Card (Please Print)

Signature

ORDER #	TITLE	PRICE	QUANTITY	ITEM TOTAL
CTLP-LPB	The Co-Teaching Lesson Plan Book	$19.95		
D7ES-LPB	7 Effective Strategies for Secondary Inclusion DVD	$129.95		
DWSI-LPB	Winning Strategies for Inclusive Classrooms DVD	$139.95		
DSIP-LPB	Demystifying Secondary Inclusion Book	$29.95		
✱ Use discount pricing below if you ordered 20 or more Co-Teaching Lesson Plan Books				
ZD7ES-LPB	7 Effective Strategies for Secondary Inclusion DVD ~~$129.95~~	$65.00		
ZDWSI-LPB	Winning Strategies for Inclusive Classrooms DVD ~~$139.95~~	$70.00		
ZDSIP-LPB	Demystifying Secondary Inclusion Book ~~$29.95~~	$15.00		
			Subtotal	
	Shipping & Handling Charges $5.00 per item. FedEx 2day or 3day delivery is available — call for details. Canadian customers please call for shipping information.			
			NY add applicable Sales Tax	
			TOTAL	

Ways To Order

CALL
Toll Free
1-800-453-7461
Monday-Friday
8 am - 5:30 pm EST

MAIL
National Professional Resources, Inc.
25 South Regent St.
Port Chester, NY 10573

FAX
914-937-9327

ONLINE
www.NPRinc.com
(See over 2,000 products)